journal for life

discovering faith and values through journal keeping

Part 1: Foundations

George F. Simons

LIFE IN CHRIST,
Division of ACTA,
Foundation for Adult Catechetical Teaching Aids,
201 E. Ohio Street
Chicago, Ill. 60611

To all whose names are
inscribed in the book of my life.

With special thanks to Betty,
Mari, Pat and Elaine who womanned
the keyboard and to the Danforth
Foundation for the freedom to work.

Copyright 1975 LIFE IN CHRIST,
division of ACTA FOUNDATION
Library of Congress Catalogue No. 75-17161
ISBN No. 0-914070-07-X
Printed and manufactured in the
United States of America

Text design and illustrations by James Bradford Johnson

Contents

Introduction

Thomas Merton, Cistercian monk. Dag Hammarskjold, Secretary-General to the United Nations. At first glance these two names, side by side, seem worlds apart. What do the cloistered religious and the man of worldwide diplomacy have in common? A closer look at their stories reveals a striking similarity. Both were men who knew how to blend contemplation and action, deep reflection and appropriate expression. Strangely, both died abroad on missions of peace and understanding, Merton having only rarely left the monastery grounds, Hammarskjold on one of his frequent international peace-keeping efforts. Merton stands out as a powerful and creative voice, a unique man among monks; Hammarskjold a statesman extraordinary for the ethical tone and sensitivity of his political interventions. Both were persons who struggled to know themselves, to sound out the meaning of events in their lives. They reflected deeply and acted decisively. Both had another thing in common — each kept a journal. Hammarskjold's diary, which he described as, "a sort of white book concerning my negotiations with myself — and with God," became in its published form the book which we know as *Markings*. Thomas Merton was a more voluminous journal keeper.

Beginning with *The Sign of Jonas,* and ending with the posthumously published *Asian Journals* the world has been treated to the rare vision of a soul at work, weighing, learning, searching. I think it is safe to say that they were both great men because of their perceptive and reflective capacities. They were able to see clearly and look deeply. Keeping a journal was one way of doing this. This little book is about journal keeping. Reading it and using it do not guarantee instant political success or contemplative greatness, but becoming acquainted with the process contained here can lead to new awareness and reflective insights. *Journal for Life* is for persons who are searching. If you are such a person, this book will introduce you to the process of journal keeping. It will provide you with a tool for learning about personal values, faith and commitment, not in an abstract or theoretical sense, but rather as they are embodied in your own life history, your own present experiences, attitudes and actions. Through journal keeping you will be introduced to an ongoing process of personal spiritual growth. You will learn approaches to self-knowledge and religious study which you can continue to use long after you have completed the initial work contained here.

What can you expect to derive from your journal? Becoming conscious of your personal religious system is in itself a process of personal growth. To the degree that you are aware of the influences which are operating on you and in you, to the extent that you become conscious of the way you see your world and act in it, to the extent you also become free either to immerse yourself in them or find alternative ways of thinking and doing. Confidence in your own development and freedom comes as you establish habits of reflection and self study and as you improve your ability to communicate to yourself and to others personal feelings and experiences. Appreciation of the diversity of other persons' experiences and values and new insights into your own can result from sharing with others.

Keeping a journal might be a step in resolving conflict which you may experience between personal and institutional religion or for that matter between yourself and any of the institutions which affect your life. It is necessary that some tension always exist here, but moments of tension can be productive if you can make of them an enriching exchange between these two dimensions of life.

There is a difference between navel-gazing and knowing what you are doing with your life. In a world of many desperate needs there is an urgency for tradition and personal energy to confront each other in ways which bring institutions and individuals into active service in meeting human needs, both spiritual and mundane. The bodies of the poor need food as desperately as the spirits of the rich. We hope the process of reflection and discussion contained here becomes for you a creative resource for effective living.

I have heard Brother David Steindl-Rast say, "Happiness follows gratitude." They are, practically speaking, inseparable. To take the sequence a step further, gratitude follows the awareness that we are the recipients, possessors, or, in some way the sharers of things seen as good. There is no more important good for us to possess than ourselves. The fundamental faith of the Judaeo-Christian tradition is in a God who creates beings as good ("And God saw that all he had made was good.") and who gives them back to themselves, redeems them, saves them for the Messianic kingdom. Yet one of the roots of our contemporary malaise is a lack of self-acceptance and self-love. On this stock grows the poisonous bloom of self-hatred that bears the fruit of violence toward self and others.

If you allow it, journal keeping can take you part of the way on a journey from possession to gratitude to happiness. You will learn some positive ways of owning your personal past and present more fully, of allowing them to become assets to rejoice in rather than burdens to be carried — or abandoned.

This first little book is subtitled "Foundations" because it contains basic introductory strategies for personal spiritual growth through journal keeping. These strategies can be used profitably over and over again. Subsequent publications are planned. These will contain further strategies for discovering personal religious history, exploring theology and scripture through personal experience, and learning about the dynamics of personal decision making in the light of ethical and social demands.

SHARE YOUR SEARCH

Because it is so easy for an individual to get stuck on a private version of reality, it is helpful to do this search with others. The materials in the book are arranged in such a fashion that they can be used by a group of persons, who want to learn journal keeping. In such a group or among friends it is possible for individuals to enlarge their own self-understanding aided by the perceptions of others. Persons whom you have learned to trust can tell you what they see and hear in what you do and say. Whether you choose to do this work as an individual or with others is a decision which you must personally make.

1

Personal Religion

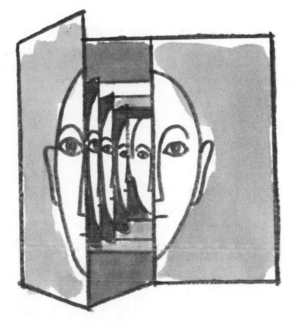

For a long time I reflected on the image of God. While I have long abandoned the "old man-white beard" kinds of imaginings, and, as a woman, have some problems with the masculine images of Father and Son, I do have a personal image of God. (God, for me is a river flowing very, very deeply within me.) Occasionally I am able to plunge down into this river, only to discover that this same river is larger than myself and flows in the rest of creation as well. Plunging into this river, I discover my deep connection not only with God but with every other being. I have a new communication and oneness with them all.

Jacqui

The question, "What is a person's religion?" can be answered in a variety of ways. We may say "He is a Christian," or "She is a Jew," meaning by this, that the person belongs to a certain class of people which is presumed to have certain common beliefs, traditions, and practices. We might go on then to describe these beliefs, traditions, and practices as a fuller explanation of that person's religion. Yet as we do this, we get farther and farther from the individual's actual experience of religion. Why is this so? Let's explore the question from personal experience.

If you were seriously asked, "What is your religion?" would you affix one of the standard labels and leave it go at that? Would you find it necessary to warn your questioner not to misunderstand, that there are, for instance, many kinds of Catholics and that you are one particular kind who believes certain things but disagrees with certain things that other Catholics might hold. There are many other people who are Catholics who see and do things differently from you, not simply those in far away lands and strange cultures. You meet them in your parish, your own community, perhaps in your husband or wife, your children or parents. Perhaps you have tried to avoid denominational differences and factions by simply labeling yourself as "Christian." Yet how many people do you find who are willing to agree with you on a common denominator of what it means to be Christian? If you share the common bond of Judaism you also experience how uncommon and diverse are its various experiences from the intensity of orthodoxy to the non-religious cultural identity of many others.

RELIGION AND YOUR RELIGION

(Today it is becoming more and more clear that the experience of religion in individuals and the institutionalization of religion in churches, teachings, practices of worship and cultural traditions, while often intimately connected, are, in reality, two quite different things.) Put simply, while it is true to say that many people "belong" to religions, it is fully and equally true to say that each person has his or her own religion. While you may or may not share a church in common with others, you nonetheless have your own unique religious history. The events which formed your set of values and religious attitudes happened in their peculiar order and intensity only to you. See how different even brothers and sisters can be even when they seem to have so much in common in their family upbringing.

If you are a member of a church or religious body, you may be aware of how you disagree with some of the things it seems to stand for or do. You may be worried about how you can honestly or wholeheartedly belong to it, worried about being hypocritical or dishonest. Even if you are in full agreement with your church, you may have anxieties stemming from the same causes. You may wonder how others who seem so different in their beliefs and practices can claim to belong to that same church. This is generally further complicated by the truth found in the statement of Wilfred C. Smith that "Normally persons talk about other people's religions as they are, and about their own as it ought to be," and, I may add, as they would like it to be.

If your church is one of those which in recent years has made serious attempts to renew itself through changes in the styles of worship, in educational techniques, and ways of decision making, you may find yourself confusedly cut off from your past, unable to communicate with your children or your parents on religious matters or even perhaps unable to live harmoniously with them because of these changes. It may make little difference whether you were one who grudgingly acquiesced to change or worked for it and welcomed it with open arms. Whether you knew it all along or only suddenly woke up to the fact, the past which you leave behind is your own past. In times of crisis its familiar comfort is harder and harder to find. It is an easy temptation to look at the past as wasted or to be angry with yourself or your teachers for what you did or learned back then in good faith which is now rejected. It is hard to be the Catholic mother of seven children when you were really hoping for only two and would have liked to have done some other things with your life. But you did it this way in real acceptance because the Church required it and now you see that same Church exercising a very practical tolerance toward birth control. Your response may be, "That's great — how I wish that had been possible for me," or you may be very angry with the clergy and laity who seem to defy traditional teaching for what appears to you as their own convenience, or you may be bitter at the Church for its inconsistency. Because the Church may have gone too far or not far enough on the particular issue which is vital for you, you may find yourself fighting it, ignoring it or leaving it.

Picking and Choosing in Religion

Nor are the Churches the powerful, all embracing social institutions they once were, capable of telling you what you can or cannot do. This power may exist in some tiny and closed communities but only to the degree that they are able to create an insulating wall between themselves and the rest of the world. Most people today find themselves for the most part living in "the rest of the world." This means that there are many sources for your values and decision making. Conflicting interests compete for your commitment, rival political parties and rival deodorants. You may find yourself choosing with reservations, selecting the candidate who seems to be the lesser of two evils, deciding how you wish to smell or whether you wish to smell. This same plurality of choices is true of religion. There are competing values not only between churches but within churches. Because churches have lost much more of their power of social con-

straint, it is possible to live in them in a kind of wary truce (between the institutional claims and your personal priorities or to ignore them altogether).
Reliable researchers point out, however, that the gap between "belonging" and
the individual's private system of belief has for most people widened even to the
point of becoming a serious breach. (We have become a supermarket society,
picking and choosing the things that work for us, that make us feel right, that we
enjoy, and passing by the things we don't need or can't find a place for.) Living
in this society, you will tend to build up a collection of values, and a set of do's
and don't's which help you to make sense out of your world and to act in a way
that you approve of. This is your actual, personal religion; and, it is true to say,
that each person has such a religion whether, to cite the extremes, it has been
mostly derived from faith handed down through the generations or whether it
has been achieved through personal acts of atheistic defiance of such faith. Thus
your personal religion may contain some things inherited and taught by your
family and church, some things absorbed from the values of society, some things
imparted in your intimate connections with others, and some things thought and
worked out of your own experiences and reflections.

Recognizing Your Religion

If this is the case, then the study of religion is not simply a matter of learning
a Church's teachings or studying about traditions and practices past or present.
These, as a matter of fact, came into existence in the first place only that you
may be helped to understand some of where you have come from, that by
reading these signposts, you may know where to search for some of the
experiences of faith that enlightened others' lives and be warned of some of the
difficulties and pitfalls which *they* experienced on the way. The pursuit (the root
meaning of the word "study") of religion includes, and perhaps especially for
adults living today, begins with the attempt to see oneself, to get a look at this
personal religion. It means inquiring into your personal history and formation,
exploring your feelings, keeping track of your present deeds, thoughts and fantasies, your reactions to events. The journal is a tool for doing this. When this
pursuit is underway, the teachings and rituals and moral demands of your tradition can possibly be reentered in a way in which they will speak saving words to
your life.

In a sense we might call the work of journal keeping a preamble to religion,
something which facilitates its emergence, a process which removes the obstacles
to our growing in religion. As such, it falls in the class of things traditionally
associated with spiritual formation and asceticism rather than with theological
research and teaching. With insights generated by modern discoveries in dis-
ciplines like psychology, education and sociology, spirituality in the 20th Cen-

tury will necessarily be different from spirituality in the 13th Century, just as that of the 13th was worlds apart from that found in the 2nd. While there is always a legitimate conservative demand for continuity in tradition, the tradition lives only as it is embodied in and borne by a succession of persons, each a product of his or her own time, each accumulating the past in a new and unique self and surpassing it.

Message carrying goes on, and yet it changes as new vehicles and media are discovered. Television does different things to us than face to face conversation; communication is there in either case, but it affects us differently. So, too, religion grows and changes as it is embodied in new persons living in different times. Thus, much of what you find here is a modern equivalent of past practice, old yet completely new. (Ways of meditation, self-examination, spiritual direction, and study are all present under contemporary forms.)

This newness of form may make it seem that there is little here that is specifically religious as you formerly understood religion. This will be particularly true if you had confined your definition of religion to the content which has been inherited from the past. It will be less true if your definition pays attention to the processes whereby religion is experienced and acquired. If you are a Christian, there is a great degree of difference between being able to mentally or verbally identify peace, patience, and meekness as Fruits of the Holy Spirit and actually knowing how and when peace, patience, and meekness emerge in your life. If you are to live increasingly in that Spirit, it is necessary to know when these things are present and what in fact encourages them and what destroys them. You ultimately need to know not in the abstract, not in someone else's account, but in the very fabric of your own life story and experience. If you are a non-believer, you nonetheless value certain qualities in your life and behavior. You have the same need to know what for you is positive and productive and what is injurious.

Thus the work proposed to you here is essentially applied philosophy or theology. Its subject matter is the process of daily living; and it leads you to know about and reflect on what you actually believe, think, do and fancy. It challenges you to bring together religion and reality, personal values and life's events, not by superimposing one on top of the other or having one vanish into the other but by taking both seriously as they work themselves out in the story of your life.

2

Keeping a Journal

Remember the ancient Greek philosopher named Socrates? He believed that, after death, people's spirits were continually reborn in new individuals. From this Socrates theorized that all learning was simply an act of remembering things which took place in a previous life. Consequently, the good teacher, for Socrates, was the clever questioner, the person adept at raising the questions which would prod people's memories into divulging what they really knew but had forgotten in the process of being reborn. For most of us, reincarnation, and belief in a former life are not a part of the way we look at ourselves. Yet, *each of us does have a previous existence* — we have a *past*. It is the place to which each instant goes as it drops over that razor's edge which divides already from not yet.

Because humans forget all too easily the events and experiences which have shaped and continue to give meaning to their lives, learning and maturation suffer. What is needed is a way of recording this flux of present into past and questioning it, forcing it to yield up the secret of who we are and what is possible to us now. Religion itself is one of the human ways of doing this. Religion, with its curious blend of personal and collective experiences, its myths and symbols, its maxims and mandates is a social manifestation of something which individuals are necessarily about whether they participate in a common faith or attempt to privatize their search as much as possible. For reasons discussed in the previous chapter, the relgious trend is moving in the direction of the private, unique and individual. Thus today, religious growth depends to a great degree on the individual's facility at getting in touch with the intensity, the succession and the flow of personal experience. Keeping a journal, because it creates an accessible record of the dialogue of inner person and outer world, has become an increasingly popular means of spiritual development. Through the ages some writers, philosophers, and saints have known the value of doing this and have kept for themselves and sometimes bequeathed to us precious journals, diaries, and notebooks. Now, in our fast moving times, when the sweeping tides of change erode familiar landmarks, it is a process that is ever more important and useful for us. The suggestions in this book seek to improve on the journal keeping process by asking stimulating questions and by using insights from our contemporary knowledge about how humans learn and mature.

RHYTHMS AND RUTS

An American philosopher once remarked that the person who does not know history is destined to relive it. So, too, if we do not know ourselves, if we do not have a perspective on our individual life history, we will find many repeating patterns developing in that life. Certainly, not all patterns are bad, but we do know what it means to say, "I get in a rut,"; "Nothing ever happens,"; "I am unhappy with my bad habits," or "I make the same mistakes over and over again." We are all too often like the man described in the New Testament epistle who looks at his face in a mirror, then walks away and forgets what he looked like. Often life's experiences, other people, our friends tell us what is happening in our lives. Sometimes we don't really allow ourselves to hear what they're telling us; at other times we nod in agreement and remember for a short while but then we go away, and since the reminder is no longer before us, we forget. Soon we find ourselves doing the same things, acting in the same way, not really having changed or grown in spite of the good information about ourselves that has come our way. Creating a written record of our experiences is one way of seeing where we have come from and learning the directions in which we want to go. Helpful rhythms and destructive patterns can both be recognized and dealt with more effectively often simply because of the increased consciousness of them which results from externalizing them in writing.

What the Journal Reveals

If you are faithful to journal keeping, you will begin to see some new things. You will see for instance how you look at the world in your own unique, personal way, how certain things are important to you and certain things not so important. You will learn what these things are. Now, I am sure that if I asked you right now what you felt was important and not important about a certain part of your life you would have some ready answers, whether they are about politics, work, child rearing or whatever; these answers would come from the conscious values which you subscribe to. This is a part of ourselves that is easy to get at and generally we are ready to admit it and speak about it. Yet the thing that so many of us desire to know about ourselves and yet are a bit afraid to look at is, How am I really doing? Am I doing well? Does what I do really correspond to what I consciously say my values are? It is important to know these things.

Being aware of the difference between my stated and lived values is in itself a fundamental step in changing my life and growing spiritually. You've probably heard it said of someone, "He or she looks at the world through rose-colored glasses." We might use the phrase to describe a person who always looks at the positive side of things that happen to him or her. This is the kind of person who is able to have energy and optimism in times when other people are perhaps overwhelmed with problems. We might ask enviously of a person like this, "where does he get this,"; "how does it work for her?" *Or,* we might ask, "What is the color of the glasses that each of *us* wears?" Indeed if we look carefully, we'll discover that each of us has a whole collection of different glasses through which we look at our world. Persons who are very concerned about financial well-being may look at just about everything through a pair of glasses which reduces the objects seen into dollars and cents. A good shopper always wears these glasses to the supermarket. A scrupulous person might look at her world through glasses which immediately see the right and wrong of every situation. One person may look at his work constantly from the viewpoint of, "how quickly can I get it done,"; "it is boring and uninteresting to me." Another person may look at her work from the point of view of how enjoyable it is, "How can I make it more enjoyable, more creative?" It is this collection of eye glasses in each individual that we call personal symbols. They are generally below the level of everyday consciousness, that is, we are usually unaware of them; they work without our really noticing that they are at work. Like the sun glasses we wear on a bright day, we forget that they are there soon after we put them on and we take for granted the colors of the things that we see. The adjustment is made in our perception and is forgotten. Just as we put on sun glasses to see better on a bright day and to prevent the sun from hurting our eyes, so, too, we generally put on our personal symbols for thoroughly good reasons. On the other hand we know how dangerous it can be if a person, while driving a car, forgets to take off those sun glasses when it begins to get dark. We also know that wearing sun glasses regularly indoors can, in the long run, affect our normal vision. So, too, our personal symbols may become so much a part of that we are no longer free to see things in different ways, and this, too, can be both dangerous and harmful.

My Symbols and Myths

In humanity's past history certain sets of symbols were possessed by whole societies of people. These symbols help people to understand their world. They allowed each individual to find his or her place in that world. Formerly, these symbols tended to evolve slowly according to the needs of the society. Today we are thrust into a rapidly moving world in which the symbol systems of societies and individuals are constantly challenged and changed by each other. We are making new symbols all the time and discarding old ones, sometimes at a frightening rate of speed. Our needs change so rapidly. Look at how quickly our political symbols come and go. The "New Frontier" soon changes to the "Great Society," and a decade later both seem like ancient history. Hair-lengths go up and down with a lot more meaning than the physical fact that a person's hair is long or short. Other symbols about the basic meaning of our lives, our religious and familial symbols may evolve less quickly, but it is even more disturbing to us when they are challenged.

When we tell a story to explain how a symbol came into being, we call that story a *myth*. Sometimes the story may be wholly fanciful in its origin, such as the story of Adam naming the animals in the Old Testament. This story is told as it is, to show humankind's superiority over and responsibility for the natural world in which we are placed. When humans look at the world with a sense of power and ownership, it is a symbol like this that they are looking through. At other times a story may be based on an actual historical event such as the story of Jesus confronting the money-changers in the temple. This story becomes a myth, however, because it becomes larger than itself. It is more than a story of a single person arguing with people he thought were doing something wrong. It has become a symbol for Christians of how piety can become corrupted with greed, and how they need always to be cautious about the connections between money and religion. Your work with your journal will help *you* to see *your* own personal symbols and myths. It will help you to identify the basic patterns through which you see life. By writing your story you will uncover the fantasies and the events, the stories which have given shape to your unique way of looking at the world. It will also help you to look at the future because you will record in it the present events, ideas, and ideals which are right now giving shape to your tomorrows.

Privacy and Sharing

As you can readily understand from what I have said thus far, the journal is essentially a personal and private thing, a mirror in which you will be able to see yourself. Diaries used to be made with locks which prevented anyone other than the owner from opening their pages. Today those locks remain on some diaries not so much as protective safeguards but as indications of the owner's desire for privacy. It is a privacy which mature adults respect in each other. Ordinarily when keeping a journal, it will be enough if you indicate this desire to the other people who are close to you. However, do whatever is necessary to gain for yourself the degree of privacy which you find necessary to work openly and honestly with yourself.

On the other hand, it is important for you to know that sharing from your journal with trusted others can be an important way of learning about yourself. By sharing from your journal with others, you come to own its contents in a new way. You admit that what you have written about yourself is truly your own. You also make it possible for others to point out to you what they see taking place in your life. Others can show you features that perhaps you have not seen or recognized and habits that are so much a part of you that you are not even conscious of them.

What I am saying here is not meant to contradict what I have just said about privacy. It is just to say that revealing yourself can be a way of growing, leaving your isolation can be a path to spiritual community, to mutual support and strength. Thus there will be times when you decide to share from your journal with friends or advisors. You may want to set aside a regular time for this with certain people, or even form a group of friends who will use the journal as a tool for personal and spiritual growth. If you do so, it is important to guard your own freedom and that of others to write what you choose by respecting each person's right to share only that which he or she chooses to share.

This respect for each other's privacy ought to be a part of an agreement of trust between friends or members of any group which chooses to use the journal as a means of growth. Sharing is always a risk but it is only by freely taken risks that we mature. Understanding that the journal is yours and yours alone to work with, to share from or not to share from, will make you free to put in it whatever is important about your own personal life and your own private reflection. There is an appendix to this book containing five brief guidelines which will be enormously helpful to you, should you choose to work with a partner or group. If you are working alone, read them anyway — they will make everyday conversation more rewarding.

3

What Goes Into the Journal?

What sorts of things might go into your journal? First of all, keep a record of significant daily events, the personal feelings that accompany them or resulted in them. Let me give you an example. Here is a recent event from my journal written on a day I spent in the hospital.

"Susan, one of my students, brought me a bag of bubble gum and a bouquet of wild flowers. She 'snuck' them up with a night nurse since I was not allowed visitors. Somehow I felt that Susan had made her whole person present to me. She is both little girl and a beautiful, powerfully caring woman who grows a little stronger each time I see her. I felt anxious about my duties as a teacher. What an awesome

responsibility to be a part of her life as she makes this exciting transition from childhood to adulthood. I felt forced to do everything possible to bring out the best of both of these parts of her."

When I reread this entry, a number of things happen to me. I become conscious of the very real affection I have for Susan — something that I cover over when I play my clergyman-teacher roles. I become aware that those roles are a set of symbols, eye glasses which tend to filter out almost everything but my sense of responsibility for others. I was looking at Susan and running her life, at least in *my* mind. I had let myself become a parent. Rather than allowing her relationship to me to become a fully adult one, I was on my way to creating the kind of relationship that she would have to back away from to be freely adult. What a tragic double loss — when I hide behind these roles, I lose the chance of meeting Susan more fully, and because I have closed myself in this way, she loses this opportunity to explore her adulthood by being treated by me as a child. Putting this entry in my journal and rereading it changes how I look at myself and at Susan. My future meetings with her are not the same. I have grown in the process of journal reflection.

REVERSING ALIENATION

Let us look at that process of growth through journal keeping from another viewpoint. The journal is a way of owning ourselves, of thoroughly possessing experiences. You might find yourself thinking as you hear me say this, "I certainly do *own* myself and all my experiences are my own, what is he talking about?" I am speaking of one of the endemic features of contemporary American society, something described in many ways, but most often called *alienation*. While over the past several years a lot of ink has been spilled about alienation in young people, it actually affects both young and old. Alienation is the result of an ingrained and highly unconscious collection of habits by which people disown their background, their history, their personal experiences, their feelings, their sense of being able to do anything about their lives or about the social, political, interpersonal and other circumstances in which their lives are lived. Individuals often give much effort to denying or covering up the neighborhood that they come from, their ethnic origin, the religious and social habits of their parents. While some of this is an expected part of the adolescent struggle for independence, for many it becomes a permanent attitude. Many persons are incapable of or at least have great difficulty in admitting their feelings to themselves or to others. Being uncertain of what my feelings imply or ask me to do, I cover them up, I don't admit to others that I have them, and quite often don't even admit their existence to myself for fear that I might have to do something about them. Ask a teenager how he or she feels about something.

Often the answer that comes back is a cryptic, "I don't know." Tragically, that which is so characteristic of the beginnings of a self-conscious emotional life on the part of a teenager is often perpetuated throughout adult life.

Tune in on the conversations around you — the very language used is often a language of alienation. I repeatedly catch myself falling into this language. Instead of speaking in the first person, I so often speak in the second person, talking about my experiences as if they were yours. See how many times in casual conversation you hear someone saying something like this, "You know, it's getting so bad that you don't know what to do any more. Whether it's politics or morals, everybody's telling you something different. You don't know who to vote for; you don't know which preacher to believe. It's no wonder your kids don't go to church and get themselves messed up on drugs and don't give a damn about being patriotic." When I hear a verbal barrage such as this I become aware of the alienation which is taking place in the communication process. The person speaking this way is not talking about *my* experience but about his or her own experience or feelings. The *you* is a bit of camouflage by which the speaker projects personal attitudes on the listener. If anyone, it is the speaker who is confused about politics and morals; it is this person's children (or the speaker's feelings about "children in general") who are freaked out and unpatriotic, not necessarily mine. Alienation in speech is so much a part of the contemporary experience that it's almost hard to notice at first — I find myself to be a frequent offender in this regard. If you do, try to catch yourself doing it. Then, switch the pronoun back to the first person. You will see how much more clear, effective and personal your communication with others becomes. If you choose to work with a group of people doing journals, you might remind each other when this alienated speech emerges. You will find some more helpful hints about effective speech in the appendix.

Your journal can help you to fight this pervading spirit of alienation. When you make entries of daily events in your journal, try to keep your description of them as graphic as possible. Write down exactly what you are feeling, seeing, hearing. Try to capture the scene in such a way that rereading it will bring it to life again. Communicating your own experiences to yourself in this way is the surest way to get meaning out of them. So many people say that their lives are meaningless and that they feel worthless. This is precisely because they actually throw their lives away by alienating their own experiences and feelings in the ways I have been talking about. It is only when I am in touch with my present and past experiences that my life is vibrant, rich and whole. This is why, incidentally, such practices as devotional confession in the Catholic Church, if practiced in the right way, can be psychologically sound and conducive to personal growth. It means owning my past, being willing to do something about it, and believing that I shall have the necessary power to carry out my willingness. On the other hand, a sure sign of stymied growth (and in its extreme form, serious mental illness) is the individual's inability to say the words "I can" when it comes to managing the course of one's life. Of course, owning one's joys and affections is as important as owning one's sins or disappointments. Both are, to use a religious term, "graces," that is, they are the features which give integrity, wholeness and beauty, we might even say "life" to human existence.

At a time when our culture virtually forbids men to cry and, some women, I think falsely, in the name of liberation, are attempting to eliminate it totally from their repertoire of human responses, we need in our own way to reappropriate what the ancient spiritual wisdom calls "the gift of tears," be they tears of sorrow or tears of joy. Life is a strong drink, meant to be drunk deeply, without being watered down.

Don't Moralize — Just Listen

When you write in your journal try not to interpret what happened or what you thought was the meaning of your feelings. Avoid the tendency to philosophize or moralize — the meaning is already there in the feeling or event as you take it to yourself as your own and record it in your journal. Moreover, if you keep a concrete record of events and feelings, you will always be able to go back to that place and live it again. On the other hand if the concrete record is missing, you will soon lose touch with what actually took place. There will be time later on to sum up what you learn about yourself. Attempting to do it prematurely frustrates the learning process.

When I look back on the diaries I kept years ago, I notice that I often did philosophize. Sometimes I have a great deal of difficulty in making sense now out of what I recorded there. I wrote such things as, "I had a most traumatic and painful encounter with Vince today." What actually took place as I remember now was that Vincent slid into home plate when I was catching and "the encounter" twisted my knee. If I were not lucky enough to remember this specific instance (I was on crutches for two months) it would be hard for me to tell whether I was talking about having an argument with someone, or bidding a dear friend goodbye. Just listen to yourself being specific about what's going on in your life— insight will follow.

Record Dreams and Fantasies

From the very start include in your journal dreams, both night dreams and day dreams, again with as much detail as you can remember. It is possible to learn and grow from your dreams and fantasies without either the extreme of ill-devised popular dream book interpretations, or, at the other extreme, the very sophisticated techniques of psychoanalysis. Dreams and fantasies will be more immediate, and easier to return to if you write them in the present tense. For example, write "I dream that I am standing in a large room. My mother enters," rather than "I was in a large room. My mother came in." Just by rereading aloud these two short examples you will get a feel for what I mean about the immediacy of the present tense. Keep in mind that everything that you dream and fantasize is a part of you. The persons and symbols that you encounter in your dreams, even though they may take their shape from actual people and events, are features of your inner landscape. Their stuff is you. Know that when you recall or reread your dreams from your journal, it is you that are learning to know better. When keeping dreams in your journal you might also note along with them actual events and encounters which seem related to them.

Other Elements

You may also include in your journal fragments of usually forgotten personal history that occur to you, those little pieces of memory which step into the light of consciousness for a moment because of some connection with a present person, place, word, or event. Note also the context in which they occur and the feelings which are the result of them. You might include in your journal cutouts or drawings, or pictures which have a particularly strong impact on you, things which you see and perhaps have some indescribable meaning or significance, some strong attraction or repulsion. Note alongside of them what feelings and thoughts they give rise to in you. Finally, your journal is your journal. It is anything you choose to record or remember. Again, try always to be as immediate and specific as possible.

The remainder of this book contains a variety of exercises which will accelerate and intensify the journal keeping process. They are special ways of asking yourself questions, of reaching hard to get parts of you, of getting vantage points for a personal perspective of your life story. Many of them can be used over and over again. With your journal they provide a kind of basic toolbox for personal growth.

When to Write

When will you write in your journal? Well, any time. If it is convenient and your journal is small enough, you might take it with you throughout the day. Jottings that are made about experiences and feelings and dreams that are still vivid are much more useful than those which are distilled by reflection or partly forgotten after a period of time. On the other hand, taking a certain time each day to write in your journal can be valuable in its own way. It can serve as a meditation, a time when the images and feelings and concerns of the day are allowed to move freely through your consciousness into the record. It may be a way of summing up the day and laying it to rest before you retire.

How to Begin

You might begin your journal by a written reflection on how you feel about writing in a journal. I remember doing this when I first began. It made me realize how very worried I am about being perfect, to be approved by others, how critical I am of myself. My first page reads,

> *"This book is me. I am afraid I am going to try to make it beautiful, to write for an audience, to hide certain things. I want to be careful not to write for an audience, the audience of criticizing voices inside of me.*
>
> *How hard it was for me to buy a book without lines! I am afraid that if the lines aren't there I will not be beautiful. What if I mess up? If the pen blots? Suppose I don't turn out well."*

Here are some questions you might ask yourself as you begin your journal:

> *If you kept a diary or journal in the past or do now, how do you feel about it? What have you learned from it? Whose life stories had had an influence on your life? What things do you think you might learn from keeping a journal, or writing your own autobiography? What things might you be afraid of in doing this?*

If you are going to do this work with others, these questions might provide the framework for your first discussion together.

There is a summary at the end of this chapter which briefly and concisely reiterates the major points about journal keeping which we have discussed thus far. *Refer to it frequently,* until you feel that you have absorbed the basic techniques.

Continued Benefits

The benefits of journal keeping are much more easily experienced than they are described. Something so simple as taking a little time out from the quick pace of everyday living to pay attention to yourself, can already seem like its own reward. But most of all the journal allows you to see yourself, to see what you need, to see how you're spending your time, to get an overall picture of things that satisfy you and the things which displease you. Through it, you will get a glimpse of the things that work and don't work for you. The process is so simple that it's deceptive. The best way to experience what I'm telling you is to try journal keeping for a couple of weeks. Most people who have tried it discover a significant difference in the way they feel about themselves. Rereading the journal at various intervals will be a growing source of insight as the pieces of your story fall into place and the total image becomes more complete.

Journal keeping is like having a wine cellar. One can always drink from it, but its finest products require patience during the aging process. Your journal can and will provide you with daily nourishment, but do not be in too big a hurry to drink it all in at once. I suggest that you begin using the following special exercises at the rate of about one a week. This will give you time to reflect on what they reveal to you and to write about your discoveries in your journal. After a while you will have your own sense of how often you want to use them and when you feel it useful to repeat certain ones.

JOURNAL KEEPING — A PRACTICAL SUMMARY

The Journal is a tool for personal spiritual growth. It functions by allowing you to get both an overall picture of yourself, your rhythms and directions, and insights into the specific events and feelings of your daily existence. It combines in itself the functions of many traditional religious exercises formerly contained in examination, meditation, and spiritual direction.

To start your journal, obtain for yourself a notebook, *preferably an unmarked, bound manuscript book.* A bound book encourages you to keep mistakes or unpleasant entries. Uncomfortable parts of yourself which emerge need to be accepted and dealt with as a part of the whole picture. It should not be too easy to throw them away. An unmarked, unlined book enables you to establish personal boundaries and style without constraints of time and space generally found in diaries.

The journal is essentially *personal* and private, a mirror in which to see yourself. Never allow yourself to be pressured into revealing its contents, although, on the other hand, you may profit from choosing at times to share from it with other trusted individuals. Personal rereading is important, perhaps the entire week at the end of the week, the month at the end of the month, later on an annual rereading, etc.

Things which your journal might contain:

a) a record of significant daily events and the personal feelings which accompanied or resulted from them. Graphic description of events and specific feelings should be emphasized rather than interpretations of what happened or what one thought the meanings of one's feelings were. Avoid the tendency to "philosophize." If a concrete record of events and feelings is missing, you will soon lose touch with what actually took place. Much potential self-understanding will be lost.

b) dreams (night or day fantasies), again with as much detail as can be remembered. They will be more immediate if written in the present tense, e.g., "I dream that I am (rather than "I was") standing in a large room. My mother enters. She is wearing a flowered hat, etc."

c) cut-outs or drawings of pictures or symbols which have particularly strong impact on you.

d) fragments of usually forgotten personal history. Little pieces of memory which step into the light for a moment. Note the context in which they occur and the feelings which call them forth or result from them.

e) the exercises which follow in this book. The journal serves as the workbook and repository in which these strategies are used. The instructions accompanying each exercise suggest the appropriate time for each to be used and indicate how the exercise might be adapted and repeated.

f) anything you choose — but again, try to be immediate and specific.

If convenient, your journal might accompany you throughout the day. *Jottings* made when experiences and *feelings are vivid* are more useful than those distilled by time. On the other hand, taking a certain time to write in the journal can serve as a meditation, a time in which images, feelings, and concerns are allowed to move freely through the consciousness into the record.

MY FEELINGS ABOUT JOURNAL KEEPING

MY FEELINGS ABOUT JOURNAL KEEPING

4

The Me I See —
Feelings and Facts

AN OPENING SNAPSHOT

The whole of your journal will be a tool for making you aware of yourself and your personal story as a resource for living. But, just to get the feel of it, this first journal exercise has been devised to provide a brief experience of what it is like to put down in front of yourself an assortment of pieces of the picture of you. The exercise is simple. It is a list of questions emphasizing religious issues but ranging far and wide, touching many matters, some important and some trivial, some very personal, others not private at all.

What Do I Look Like?

Every morning I face the bathroom mirror and I check out my face. This is the only picture of myself which I ordinarily see. I am used to it. It rarely surprises me. Then on occasion another picture appears, candid and revealing. It may be a snapshot made by a friend — I am in the middle of doing something or saying something. It may be in the multiple mirrors of a department store where I see myself from the side, or the back. There is a rush of emotion which accompanies this unfamiliar vision of myself, an uncertainty about this other me. I suspect that it is this feeling which makes people hide from cameras or be terribly self-conscious when photos are being taken. I have heard it said that certain "primitive" people refuse to be photographed because they feel that the picture will capture their spirit and carry it off. I am one of those "primitives." It is the same feeling which makes me pose in front of a camera, all not to be caught by surprise. Either I want a very controlled, attractive image or one so ridiculous that no one takes it seriously as me.

Yet the me that I am embarrassed about looking at, the angle that reflects the me I rarely see, is probably the me that others are looking at all the time. While I walk about under the illusion of what I look like to me, others are seeing more and different things. Moreover, my eye is selective even with what it does see. When I step from my morning shower, I may focus on my bicep and ignore my paunch, or I may focus miserably on my paunch and ignore the expressiveness of my eyes.

All of this says that a lot more information about me is available to me than I ordinarily seek out or use. Knowing what I choose to see and what I choose not to look at tells me what I think of myself. Likewise what I choose to reveal or hide from others tells me more about the person I am.

Looking at who I really am and accepting that picture is a starting place for personal growth. I am what *I* have to work with. I am my primary resource. This truth can at once be the hardest and most useful fact for my personal future. It is the hardest because others (in the struggle to rise) have so often put me down that I have learned to do it for myself. I have been carefully taught to see the bad, inadequate, inferior me and to feel miserable and incapable because of it.

Keeping a journal is geared to help you look at yourself in a new way, that is, as yourself, not as miserable or great, but as you, a unique combination of inside and outside, a once for all constellation of past experiences and present thoughts and feelings, a life always in the making, being constructed of that you which exists now, bearing within it all that has been accumulated and experienced so far. With this view you can, hopefully, grow without the paralysis of a poor self-image or the equally debilitating philosophy that leads me to believe that I am always and ever "O.K."

Here Are the Questions

   Answer each of the following questions in your journal briefly, that is, with a full sentence or two at most. It will be helpful if you include the question in the answer, so that you will know precisely what you are talking about then you reread your snapshot in the future.

   How important in your life is religion?
   What is the source of your financial income?
   How religious were your parents?
   What is your favorite hobby or leisure interest?
   Were you born into a religion? Did you acquire one or leave one?
   What do you feel most proud of / ashamed of in your past?
   How satisfied are you with your present religious position? How would you want to change it? If you were to change religions, which would you choose?
   What is your grade point average at present? Your average income?
   What social class do you see yourself belonging to?
   Have you ever cheated on exams? In business?
   How do you feel toward a person whose religious convictions forbid him / her to smoke? Drink? Dance? Cooperate with selective service or serve in the military? Hold public office? Engage in extra- or pre-marital sexual acts? Travel overseas? Use mechanical and chemical farming methods? Eat certain foods? Kill animals? Cut down trees? Turn away strangers? Work on holidays? Gamble? Let his wife be seen in public?
   What is the most serious lie you have ever told?
   Are your religious beliefs an aid or a hindrance to your freedom? How?
   If you would be anyone / thing — besides yourself — who / what might it be?
   How do you like your name?
   What do you like most / least about being male / female?
   Have you any health problems? What are they?
   Have you ever had a mystical experience? What was it like?
   What do you regard as the chief fault in your personality?
   Have you ever been arrested or fined for violating any laws?
   What do you get most excited about?
   What kills your enthusiasm the quickest?
   What sins do you feel most guilty about?

Do you have religious anxieties about asking / answering questions such as these?

What do you regard as your least / most attractive physical features?

Are you or your parents divorced? Have you ever considered divorce?

What person would you most like to take a trip with right now?

Have you ever been tempted to kill yourself? Someone else?

What is your fantasy about God?

Would you participate in a public religious demonstration?

What emotions do you find it most difficult to control?

How often do you pray? To whom? How often do you attend religious services? Where?

What emotions are you feeling right now?

What image do you remember from a recent dream? What feeling?

What is your IQ?

What are you most reluctant to write about now?

Have you ever been involved in a homosexual encounter?

Who is your religious counselor? Your favorite religious personage?

What career goals do you have?

Have you ever experienced premarital or extramarital sex?

How do you feel about crying in the presence of others?

Do you use tobacco, marijuana, alcohol, drugs?

At present, what is your greatest ethical dilemma?

What were you most praised and liked for as a child?

What were you most punished or criticized for as a child?

What is the subject of your most frequent daydreams?

What foods do you most like / dislike? TV programs?

Is there a person you wish would be attracted to you? Who? (Give name.)

What has been your most unpleasant experience with religion?

What is the subject of the most serious quarrels you have had with your parents? With your husband or wife?

*How could you improve your present living arrangements? ***

* These questions are adapted from J. William Pfeiffer and John E. Jones (Eds.) *A Handbook of Structured Experiences for Human Relations Training,* Volume III, pp. 92-93 (Rev.). La Jolla, Ca.: University Associates Publishers, 1974. The University Associates Version was itself an adaptation of guidelines which appeared in Jourard, S.D., Disclosing Man to Himself (Princeton, N.J.: Van Nostrand, 1968).

Perhaps, as you thought about these questions, others occurred to you. If so, jot them down and answer them. They will help you to fill out this picture of yourself.

QUESTION:

QUESTION:

QUESTION:

QUESTION:

QUESTION:

QUESTION:

QUESTION:

QUESTION:

QUESTION:

Studying Your Snapshot

When you have finished, reread your answers once or twice.

Who is the you that emerges?
What do you look like as you see yourself from these angles?
How do you feel about what you see?
Jot down your feelings and reactions in your journal.
How do you see your picture, as mostly positive or negative?
Can you begin to see each of these parts of you as an asset, a resource, a starting point useful for your present and future growth?
Were there questions that you found difficult to answer or answer honestly even in the privacy of your own journal?
Did you find yourself about to put down your usual public answers for some of these questions but then feeling that those answers were less than adequate for your private self?
Did you discover that you kid yourself about some things?

These discoveries are an indication of places where you have a potential to grow. Just seeing them clearly is already a good part of growing.

Include in your journal the observations which you make about your snapshot (page 29).When you have finished this exercise, you will have completed one mental and emotional picture of yourself. Many others are possible. Be on the lookout for provocative questions. Get in the habit of answering for yourself the questions that you want to or actually do ask of others.

Actual Photographs

There is learning in actual photographs, too. If you have some photos of yourself, you might add them to your journal at least jotting down the feelings and ideas that they give rise to as you look at them (page 28). Once when I began a physical fitness class, the instructor insisted that we begin by being photographed as we were in full length, front, side, and back views, with a Polaroid camera he had brought with him. His intention was to photograph us at the end of the program and by comparison show the changes we had made in posture, weight and tone. Being photographed in my shorts, unposed, all of me, and later pasting these photos side by side in my journal was an experience accompanied by a variety of emotions, which as I allowed them to emerge, taught me much about my attitudes toward myself, my self-image. If you decide to use actual photos in your journal, get some new ones made if possible. Note your personal reflections on the photos. Write about them. What was it like to be photographed? What feelings emerged when you first saw new snapshots of yourself? Write about these feelings too.

A Self Portrait

Another exercise frequently used with children is drawing a picture of one's self. You don't need to be an artist. Perhaps it's best if you're not. Just draw it in your journal as you feel it coming (page 28). When you've finished, jot down your feelings toward the drawing. Answering these questions for yourself will yield some further insights. Which part of me have I drawn with greatest / least detail? Which parts of the drawing do I like most / least? Where have I deliberately exaggerated or departed from how I actually see myself?

The ancient philosopher said, "Know thyself." This task begins with another, "See thyself." Knowing one's self can only be the product of repeated in-depth views of the self. Snapshots and portraits yield some initial views. As you continue your journal, you will discover and learn to invent for yourself new angles from which to comprehend yourself.

Getting a picture of yourself has deep spiritual and religious significance. Distorted images, estimates of the self which are inflated or deflated or just not factual are shaky foundations for the spiritual life. Humility and truth have often been equated in religious literature. But, what truth can there be without observation, without taking frequent looks at ourselves, without continuing to look from new vantage points?

Working With Others

If you have chosen to begin your journal work with friends or in a learning group, you may use this exercise in quite a different way. Break your group into pairs and find a private place for each pair of persons to converse. In your pair take turns for about an hour asking each other questions from the list in this exercise. Most likely there are questions on the list that you would not like to answer in front of someone else or shared beyond the confines of your conversation with your partner. Therefore, you are to strictly observe three ground rules in your discussion:

One—WHAT YOU SHARE WITH EACH OTHER IS TO BE KEPT STRICTLY CONFIDENTIAL BETWEEN THE TWO OF YOU. If you discuss this exercise later in your larger group, talk only about the experience, not about the content of your private exchange.

Two—ASK NO QUESTIONS OF YOUR PARTNER THAT YOU WOULD BE UNWILLING YOURSELF TO ANSWER.

Three—FEEL FREE TO DECLINE TO ANSWER ANY QUESTION THAT YOU FEEL UNCOMFORTABLE ABOUT. NO REASONS NEED BE GIVEN.

PASTE
SNAPSHOT
HERE

SELF-PORTRAIT
HERE

In addition to getting a picture of yourself (you may answer the questions in your journal before sharing them or after if you choose)·doing this exercise with another or in a group helps you to discover the degree of privacy which you are comfortable with and the limits of your ability or desire to share with others.

OBSERVATIONS

5

Ups and Downs

Life is punctuated with sweet moments and sour ones, acceptance and rejection, growth and diminishment. In homey language, I talk about my "ups and downs," my "highs and lows." I walk through my everydays like a hiker, on occasion looking down from the peak of some great experience or discovery, sometimes looking up from a low valley of disappointment or hurt. Often, however, I am climbing or slipping, being little aware of much more than the terrain which immediately surrounds my feet. Sometimes I suspect I'm even traveling around in circles, not sure that I'm going any place at all or in the direction I desire. This is particularly true in what we describe as the religious aspects of our lives. There are moments of belief and doubt, times of confidence and confusion, periods of sin and grace, mystical moments. These parts of life are the very fabric of our religious existence and, for this reason, we deserve to look very carefully at what they tell us about ourselves.

This exercise is a structured way of helping you to view your religious ups and downs. It will give you an overall picture of the high and low points of your personal religious experience and, in addition, provide you with a tool to study other factors, fluctuations in other areas of your life which are related to and affect who you are religiously.

RELIGIOUS EXPERIENCE GRAPH

The graph is a dynamic way of charting ups and downs. If you think of the graphs displayed on the finance pages of the newspaper, you will recall how the zigzag lines or vertical blocks record the ups and downs, the highs and lows of sales, production or profits. In this exercise, the graph is used as an index of the highs and lows of religious experiences in an individual's life. There is such a graph on page 32. It reflects how one person saw the important events in his inner life and recorded them. Study it for a few moments. What kind of feel does it give you for this person's life? What is the texture of your own experience? The empty graphs printed on page 35 and 36 are places for you to make such a record of the religious events in your own history. You may copy the graph on a page of your journal, or work here and transfer it later. Notice the starting point in the middle of the left side of the graph. Experiences recorded above the middle line would be ones you feel positive about, the high points, important insights, events and encounters which helped you grow, while those below would be negative ones, times you felt stifled, injured, diminished in your religious life. Draw a line which reflects your own religious experiences. As you move from left to right, you will be going from the time of your birth to the present.

Depending on your age, let the individual blocks of the graph stand for a year or two or three. The line zigzagging up and down will indicate the high and low points of your religious experience *as you see them* now. Mark a word or two at each peak and valley on your graph to indicate to yourself what actual experience they refer to. Some such points might be: "First Communion," or "loss of my faith," or "my husband's death." They might mark encounters with the important people in your life, ideas which changed your goals, or your belief about them. Whatever it is, try to find that which is actually important for you, not what others have said is "supposed" to be important.

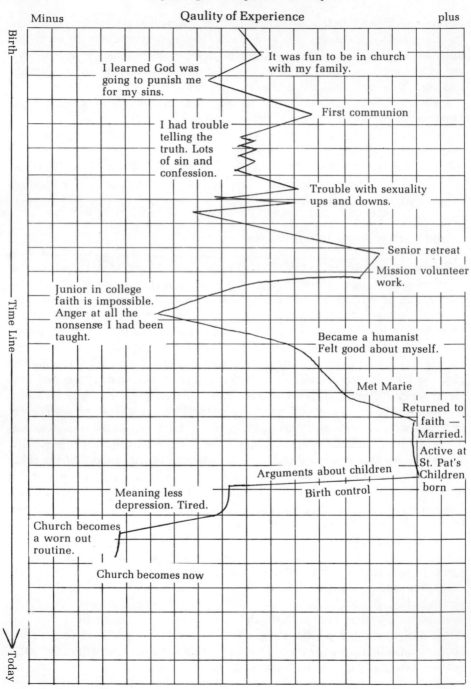

Minus   Qaulity of Experience   plus

Birth

Time Line

Today

It was fun to be in church with my family.

I learned God was going to punish me for my sins.

First communion

I had trouble telling the truth. Lots of sin and confession.

Trouble with sexuality ups and downs.

Senior retreat

Mission volunteer work.

Junior in college faith is impossible. Anger at all the nonsense I had been taught.

Became a humanist Felt good about myself.

Met Marie

Returned to faith — Married.

Active at St. Pat's Children born

Arguments about children

Birth control

Meaning less depression. Tired.

Church becomes a worn out routine.

Church becomes now

Learning From the Graph

When you have finished your graph to your satisfaction, take some time to look carefully at it. Jot down what you discover and the feelings which result from it. When you have done this, here are some questions which might provoke further written reflection in your journal:

What does your graph tell you about your religious experiences? Are they predominantly high or low? Are there some parts of your life which are more satisfying religiously speaking than others?

Can you see any patterns which repeat themselves? Are there certain kinds of experiences which are more satisfying or disturbing than others?

Which things would you like to experience again? Which would you not like to experience again?

Who are the important persons whose lives intersect with yours in the graph? What roles did they play in your experiences? Do you feel that their influence was positive or negative?

What consequences for spiritual growth do you see? Does your graph give you some expectations or anxieties for the future?

Repeated Use of the Graph

The graph is a tool which you can use repeatedly in your journal. You don't need special graph paper to do so. Simply draw a horizontal line to mark the center, then draw your experience line from left to right as going above or below as far as seems right for each experience. Mark each peak or valley with the name of the event or encounter which it represents.

If you make a habit of writing daily in your journal, making a *graph of the day's activities* or its highs and lows is a good way to get in touch with the significant things that you want to enter into your journal for that day. Similarly, a *graph for the week* would be important in a lengthier perspective.

It is also valuable to do more life pictures like the religious experience graph, views of *various aspects of your personal history* from the beginning to the present. These might include high and low points in:

relationships with others
career
feelings about your body
satisfaction with yourself
sexual experience
financial well being
health and / or physical fitness
personal popularity
sin and grace as you felt them.

You will probably think of dozens more. Insights can result not only by reflecting on the individual graphs but also by comparing them with each other. You might begin to see which phases of your life are related to each other, which gave you greatest or least satisfaction, which parts of your life are out of step with the others. Seeing more of yourself in this way, you will begin to make better decisions for your future.

A Shared Exercise

If you are working with a partner or a group, you can study your graph work together. Talk about the experience of drawing the graph, what it felt like and what you learned. If you choose to show your graphs to each other or describe parts of them, you might use the questions above as a starting point for your discussion.

For a variation on this experience, you might ask a member of your group who knows you well, a friend, relative or spouse to draw one of the suggested graphs about you as he or she sees you. Compare this line with the one you drew yourself about the same phase of your experience. Discuss the differences. What new insights emerge?

Friends or spouses can use the graph together to chart what they see as the ups and downs in their mutual relationship. By comparing perceptions they can use this graph as a means to grow in understanding and occasionally as a way of resolving tensions and disagreements.

The experience graph is a basic strategy for personal growth. In addition to the suggestions we have discussed, you will probably be able to invent many more graphs that are useful to you. Happy plotting!

6

The Inner Exchange

A. Why don't you stop being such a disagreeable person? You just hurt Helen very much with your anger and cutting remarks.

B. I don't know. I just can't help myself. She's so nice to me that I feel smothered by her kindness and something in me just rebels and I feel this uncontrollable anger welling up inside.

A. Don't you know that anger is a sin? It's coming from that un-disciplined bad side of you that you don't seem to want to do anything about.

B. Now you're sounding like my mother. I really don't know whether I'm doing right or wrong. My real feelings are struggling with what my conscience says. Sometimes I feel right and other times I feel so guilty. . .

Terry

Listening to the inner exchange can become one of the most useful exercises for your on-going personal journal work. In the very conversations of your mind lies a resource capable of exploring any issue you choose. When your mind converses with itself each different part of you has a voice of its own. In this exercise all that you have to do is listen in and capture what is said. Reflecting on your inner exchange will tell you much about yourself.

WHAT ARE THESE VOICES ALL ABOUT?

Sometimes I hear voices. There are arguments going on inside of me. Some have been going on for years now, most of the time deep below the surface of my conscious life, but from time to time surfacing when I need to make a decision or perhaps causing me a sleepless night. I may be thinking of buying something and am uncertain about whether I'm getting too materialistic. I wonder about how well I am doing my job, whether I should spend more time in prayer, whether I should pay more attention to my body's needs for rest and exercise, and so on and on.

Often questions never get resolved because I never get all the issues out in front of myself. I let my memory play tricks on me or I choose not to listen to some parts of the argument as much as to others. I confuse pressures and feelings coming from inside of myself with those coming from outside — for example, I may fear displeasing a friend by asking that person to go to church with me. The fear may be my own ambivalence about professing my faith to another rather than the other's actual displeasure. When I recognize my own internal fear, I can more freely ask of the other what I want. I may be surprised at the other's willingness to do just what I was afraid to ask about. Even if my friend refuses or is displeased, I can recognise the difference between my own fears and the other person's actual reaction. You may also get a picture of the relative value with which you hold certain things.

When I recognize the existence of this inner exchange within myself, I begin to see clearly that there are different parts of me looking for different things. I will learn how to care for my needs more effectively.

How to Listen In

Set aside a little quiet time. Then, in a comfortable place, close your eyes and allow yourself to get in touch with some area of uncertainty or some unfinished decision inside of you. It may be a question of faith which you find difficult to resolve; it may be hesitation over the morality of something you are planning to do, the goodness or evil in some impending decision or action. When a subject of importance for you emerges, allow an exchange to take place within your mind on this subject. I'm sure you are familiar with the kind of exchange I mean. It's the sort of discussion or argument that goes on when you are trying to make a decision and one part of you says don't do it for such and such reasons, and another part of you says — yes, but maybe I can do it for such and such reasons. So the dialogue goes on. Listen to the dialogue in you about the specific subject that you have chosen, and, as that dialogue develops, record it in your journal.

Don't try to create an imaginary theater piece. Just let the voices emerge and write down what they say. Twenty minutes to half an hour will generally be plenty of time for all the major arguments to surface on both sides of a question.

Learning From the Inner Exchange

When you have finished, reread what you have written carefully and slowly aloud to yourself. Just hear what is going on. Next, with each character take a few moments to look at it a second time. Reread the exchange once again. Do you hear anyone's voice there besides your own? Or, if you expressed the dialogue calling one side "I" and the other "You," reverse the pronouns as you read it the second time.

Here are some questions that may be helpful to you as you reflect on your inner exchange and comment on it in your journal.

> *How did you feel while doing this exercise?*
> *What did you discover about yourself?*
> *Did any of the voices in your exchange sound familiar, e.g., father, mother, friend, teacher, etc.? Do you find that voice stronger or weaker than the other?*
> *Did you discover anything by reversing the "I" and "you" roles in the dialogue?*
> *How do you feel about your predicament now as you see both sides written out in front of you? Does the problem seem larger or smaller, changed in any way?*
> *Which side was winning? Were you pleased or angry, etc., about the way it was turning out? Which side was harder to listen to?*
> *How do you feel about accepting both sides or voices as legitimate parts of you?*
> *Did you suppress any part of the emerging dialogue?*

Use Frequently

Experiencing, recording and listening to the dialogues which go on within us can become a rewarding habit, a regular method for drawing understanding and strength from the inner exchange. It is a procedure which you can use again and to become more aware of the conflicting influences in your thinking, the values and beliefs you worry about, the rationalizations you fear you may be making in your moral life. Thus, listening in and re-sorting is like taking an aerial photograph. You are given a vantage point from which you can reconnoiter the inner struggles and deployment of energies for decision making and maturation. Exchanges can take place repeatedly, continuing unresolved questions or moving on to different issues.

It is possible to create an exchange not only with both sides of an argument going on in you (decision making), but with virtually any one or any thing which has been a significant part of your experience or even of your fantasy. You may speak with your body or parts of it, with parents, friends, acquaintances, with important moments in your personal history, past and to come (birth, marriage, death), with feelings (anger, desire, pleasure), with your activities, job, hobbies, etc. If something is important to you, you can engage in an exchange with it.

Here are some exchanges you might consider doing. I'm sure you will think of many others:

Between the "I would like to" and the "I should" parts of myself.
With Jesus or another traditional religious figure.
With a contemporary religious figure, e.g., my pastor, etc.
Discussion with the high and low point events on your religious experience graph or other graphs.

Remember that each part, each voice in the discussion is a feature of yourself. Keep this in mind as you reread what you have written. As you do this, you are coming to possess various fragments of yourself more securely by capturing them in your journal. Even though one of the speakers in the exchange may bear someone else's name, e.g., "my mother" or seem to be an external event, e.g., "my husband's illness," keep in mind that you are not in dialogue with the person herself or the event itself, but each of these as it is contained in the storehouse of your personal perceptions, memories, and feelings. Each is a part of you that you need to be fully aware of as belonging to you, locating in it the repertoire of your available energies, owning it as a resource in your internal growth process.

Sharing the Inner Exchange

If you are doing your journal work with someone else, in addition to the questions raised above, here are some things you might like to tell each other about:

Which side seemed more convincing?
What seemed to be the blocks which prevent the dilemma from being resolved?

> *What side of the argument seemed more like the you that others know?*
>
> *Did any statements seem like rationalizations?*

Raise any questions which seem important about the opinions which you receive.

Remember, what each offers is an attempt to be helpful. It is the expression of a way in which the other sees you. It is not necessary to defend your position if you have another interpretation for your thinking or behavior.

What is important is that you allow the exchange to emerge from the voices inside you. Freedom from distracting influences and some initial quiet reflective moments before writing will be enormously helpful.

A tape recorder may be useful for learning from your exchange. Read the dialogue into the recorder and play it back for yourself.

AN INNER DIALOGUE

VOICE 1

VOICE 2

VOICE 1

VOICE 2

VOICE 1

VOICE 2

AN INNER DIALOG

VOICE 1

VOICE 2

VOICE 1

VOICE 2

VOICE 1

VOICE 2

VOICE 1

VOICE 2

7

Canonization: The Human Being Hall of Fame

We have already alluded to the importance of a constructive self-image as a solid basis and energy source for growth and maturation in the spiritual life. Early in the process of journal keeping, it is extremely useful to take an overall look at the state of optimism which we have about ourselves and our religious life. It is important to see how we look at what we have done with our lives thus far and how we expect to grow, what the past has been and what we anticipate the future to be. *Canonization: the Human Being Hall of Fame* is an ingenious way to explore what we perceive to be our personal religious strengths and weaknesses.

Perhaps you are familiar with the canonization process of the Roman Catholic Church. Not too many years ago it was the subject of a best selling novel called The Devil's Advocate. In the canonization, which is like a trial, two men act as lawyers arguing against each other — one arguing for the holiness and worthiness of the deceased person to be proclaimed a saint — the other arguing against it. In our exercise you will be the candidate for sainthood or for inclusion in the Human Being Hall of Fame. Since you have an intimate acquaintance with the subject, you will also play the roles of both lawyers.

HOW TO CANONIZE YOURSELF

Based on what you know about yourself now, write in your journal a short autobiography, only a couple of pages long, about your life. You may do it in either of two ways, either by using only what you know about your life up until this time; or, by using both that information, and, then carrying your life into the future by fantasizing how you expect your life to turn out based on what you already know about yourself. Imagine that what you are writing is a lawyer's argument, a brief, prepared to argue for your sanctity, holiness, greatness or goodness. Its object is to convince those who read it that, without question, you should be declared a saint, or a great human being, a person whose life was a triumph, a model and inspiration for others. Call attention to your good points and achievements. Stress things that other people like about you and appreciate in you. If you are using the second form, projecting into the future, put in some of your future accomplishments and the life style that makes you a good and successful person. You might terminate the story with how your death — perhaps even martyrdom — declared your holiness and wholeness as a person. Then, when you have completed this first brief, write another one using the same narrative thread of your life which you chose the first time, writing about yourself either up to the present or projecting into the future. But now, using what you know about yourself, you are writing the role of the devil's advocate. This new brief argues against your sanctity. Consequently, you describe all your bad points, you pick upon all the bad aspects or motives hidden even in the events you argued positively for in the first brief. Give events your own most unfavorable interpretation. Take about an hour to write both sets of arguments.

Processing the Canonization

When you have completed both sets of arguments, read them over carefully. If possible, do it aloud and convincingly, as if you were arguing them in front of the jury which was about to rule on their merits and pass judgment. (Another way to do this is to read them into a tape recorder and then allow yourself to be the jury as you listen to the playback of the arguments.) Listening to yourself is the most important part of this exercise. Permit what you hear about yourself, positive and negative, to sink in. Recognize the feelings which come to the surface as you do this. What are they? Joy, fear, satisfaction, despair? Are these ways that you usually feel about yourself?

You may learn more about this experience of reviewing the case for and against your holiness, goodness and greatness by journal writing. Here are some evocative questions which will be of use to you as you proceed:

> *Describe how you felt while writing the briefs. Which was harder to write? How did you feel while reading them?*
>
> *How do you feel about having several possible interpretations about the meaning and value of your life?*
>
> *Which brief is most believable to you, the one for your inclusion or the one against it? How do you feel about this?*
>
> *Were there areas that you found while writing which were more difficult to deal with than others? Did you find yourself deliberately suppressing certain ones. What were they?*

Working With Others

If you are working with a friend or a group, you may discuss the previous questions and also share your briefs in part or in full. If so, read them aloud and convincingly as if you are really arguing the case before a court.

> *How does it feel to read these arguments?*
>
> *Have the listener(s) decide which brief was more convincing. Ask another to point to the strongest features of the winning and losing sides and to the things he or she found more interesting or noteworthy in your presentation. Compare the other's choices with your own estimate of what was most important to you.*

Canonization Can Be Repeated

Like the Experience Graph and the Inner Exchange, this Canonization exercise can be repeated. It is a reusable tool. Obviously, the form that you have just used will be helpful only at greater intervals (e.g., annually, perhaps around your birthday) when you wish to check out overall changes in how you view yourself. However, an abbreviated version can be useful more often for exploring individual events and encounters with others. Write about what took place twice, the first time giving the best possible interpretation to your involvement in the encounter or event, the second time giving your most unfavorable understanding to your motives, words and actions, etc. As in the original exercise, reread the two descriptions and listen to your feelings toward each. Ask yourself questions similar to the ones used for the canonization exercise. Assess whether you feel differently toward yourself or the event as a result of doing this exercise.

THE CASE FOR MY CANONIZATION

THE CASE AGAINST MY CANONIZATION

8

Windows on God

Windows on God is an exercise which will help you recognize your interior condition regarding the issue and person of God. It is directed toward your personal conception of God, your experiences with God, first as someone you learned about, secondly as the object of your own experience, and finally in terms of what you want to learn about God and do about God in your life. All of these perspectives are directed toward answering for yourself the question, "Who is your God?".

Often what an individual has been taught, what an individual has learned by experience, and what that same person's expectations are regarding one thing are quite different from one another. For example, a person may have been taught that (1) people who do not work are good for nothing. The same person finds (2) that in actual experience his/her present occupation is demeaning and unpleasant, yet he or she (3) hopes that work will be a prime source of personal satisfaction in life. Each of these three perceptions is challenged by the others. By placing them side by side, the individual is allowed to see and own the conflicting parts of his or her own attitudes about work. Whether these conflicts can be resolved by certain decisions or actions on the part of the individual depends on this clear recognition of what makes up the individual's interior condition regarding the issue.

CONSTRUCTING THE WINDOWS

Make yourself comfortable and begin using a pen or pencil to divide a page of your journal paper in half with a straight horizontal line, and then in quarters with a straight vertical line down through the middle. Your page should now look like an old-fashioned window with four panes to look through (page 51). You are going to fill in three of these panes with drawings, symbols, or words. In the first pane, create a visual representation or written summary of God as God has been presented to you or taught to you. Here you might indicate what your parents passed on to you, what you heard in Sunday School, Church, a religion or theology class, etc.

In the second pane, create an image of God as you have known him through your own experiences or your personal searching. This may be an attempt to portray or describe moments when you felt His presence or closest to Him. It may portray the darkness and confusion of your search for Him — whatever your own personal experience has been.

In the third pane, depict God as you would like to know Him, your vision of what God ought to be or might be in your life, or how you might personally want to resolve the question of God's existence or God's demands on you, whatever you would like to do or know about God. Leave the final pane empty. You will use it for making notes later on.

Reflecting on What You See

When you have finished the three panes, study your drawing for a while. Then in the empty pane, jot down whatever strong feelings, impressions, or resolutions which emerge from what you see. Note what naturally occurs to you as you look at the juxtaposition of the three perspectives. Avoid forcing conclusions.

Learning Together

If you are sharing your work with another, you might allow that person to write in the empty pane the feelings, perceptions, or questions which your three windows give rise to. Discuss these together, then note in your journal what you experienced and learned while doing this.

Clarifying Positions With the Window Strategy

God need not be the only subject of this exercise. Windows can be used repeatedly as a quick and simple strategy for clarifying personal positions both regarding explicitly religious issues as well as more secular concerns. The power of this exercise comes from the fact that it sets in clear, side by side, contrast the external influences, personal experiences and needs or expectations. By using this strategy, you are in effect asking yourself the three critical questions for a good decision: What have I learned from others? What has my experience taught me? What am I looking for, what do I really want right now? Confusion is often the result of the conflict between two or more of these elements. Placing them side by side is a particularly effective way to clarify a belief, value or decision. Use it when the question in front of you is: "What do I believe about —?" or, "What do I think I should do about —?" Some topics pertaining to your personal growth and spiritual life that you might like to explore in this fashion are: *Church, Salvation, Sexuality, Spirituality, Prayer, Work, Vocation, Marriage, Poverty.* I am sure that you will think of many more areas of religious and personal interest.

GOD AS GOD HAS BEEN PRESENTED TO ME OR TAUGHT TO ME.	GOD AS I HAVE KNOWN GOD THROUGH MY OWN EXPERIENCES OR SEARCHING.
GOD AS I WOULD LIKE TO KNOW GOD, OR, WHAT I WOULD LIKE TO DO OR KNOW ABOUT GOD.	USE THIS SPACE FOR FEELINGS, PERCEPTIONS, QUESTIONS OR RESOLUTIONS WHICH EMERGE FROM REFLECTION ON THE FIRST THREE WINDOW PANES.

9

Religious Belonging

When keeping a journal, it is good from time to time to try to summarize what you have come to know about yourself, to take stock of your present attitudes and thus to clarify which are the unresolved issues that you might want to begin to deal with in the near future. In this exercise we will raise three basic questions to help you gain some perspective on your individual relationship to religion, to allow you to see how your religion serves you, bothers you and what attitudes you take because of it.

HERE ARE THE QUESTIONS

1) As I look on my present, what are some aspects of my religion that I find useful and desirable, growth producing? List the three or four most significant.

2) As I look on my present, what aspects of my religion do I find frustrating, uncomfortable, embarrassing, inhibiting? Again, list the three or four that stand out most clearly.

3) What things do I get out of my present religious attitude? Am I a deep believer, casual adherent, questioner, agnostic, searcher, etc.? How would I best be described? What does this attitude contribute to how I feel about myself right now?

Not Judgment But Vision

Recall that when we began our journal work, we talked about snapshots and reflections. It will be helpful now to return to those analogies. The three questions about religious belonging encourage you to gather together pieces of information available to you in the various pictures of yourself which you have recorded thus far in your journal. Our assumption here is that a substantial amount of personal spiritual growth will occur if we can see clearly who we are and what it is that we do.

These introductory exercises in journal keeping avoid attempts at making you interpret, analyze or judge yourself or your behaviour. They try only to have you see yourself, your feelings, your ideas and your acts from as many honest perspectives as possible, to lead you to the best possible vision of who you really are. You will notice that the question "Why?" never appears in the course of any of the exercises you have done. It is rarely a productive question. More often it leads to excuses, defenses and rationalizations.

Most specifically it leads to the subtle confusion between subjective and objective thought. If when asked why I go to church, I answer, "Because it's the right thing to do." I avoid entirely the issue of facing my own motives which in this case may be, alternatively, a deep sense of love for my Church, fear of punishment if I do not go, acquiescence to the desires or pressures of my family, etc. There are many possibilities. Personal spiritual growth and productive sharing with others are much more likely to occur when I ask questions like: "What an I doing?", "What is taking place?", "How do I feel about it?", "What are you experiencing?"

The auxiliary verb "should" implying obligation is also absent. This does not mean that we do not contract debts and obligations, rather that we tend to accumulate too many of them. Our spiritual life becomes jailed in a kind of debtors' prison when our ability to respond gets locked up by our feeling responsible for too many things. Guilt and feelings of inadequacy immobilize even or perhaps especially the most sensitive of us. To function effectively and mature spiritually frequently means getting out from behind the "shoulds" which bar us from true affection, enthusiasm and freedom of choice.

Doing the Exercise

Copy the questions in your journal. Answer the first before copying the second. Do them this way, one at a time, answering each question as fully as possible before moving on. Remember that the first two questions ask for three or four aspects of your religion.

Here-and-Now Concrete Answers

Try to answer these questions as specifically as you can. Respond in terms of your own present feelings and concrete experiences, e.g.,

Question 1   Instead of *"The Mass is a worthwhile experience,"* write, *"I feel particularly enriched by the celebration of the Eucharist at St. Anselm's. The contemporary hymns usually speak to my feelings and I feel supported by my pastor and other members of the community there . . ."*

Question 2   Instead of, *"Clergymen tend to be overbearing,"* — *"I tend to feel guilty and manipulated when my minister preaches about prayer. I find that the prayer and moral attitudes he recommends are practices which would be false for me and hypocritical, and since I don't have personal alternatives, I feel like an outsider, empty and deficient . . ."*

Question 3   Instead of, *"I presently consider myself an agnostic,"* — *"I do not disbelieve in God, rather I am quite uncertain about what to believe. I grew up with a traditional image of God which no longer makes sense. I can no longer keep that image. Yet I have nothing with which to replace it. I do not know what to call my search for meaning or whether it should go in me or beyond me. Being an agnostic leaves me breathing space, allows me to work at these questions at my own pace, without being preached at by others or by my own conscience. I feel good about my decision to be this way because I think it is an honest reflection of my present state of personal maturity . . ."*

Reflecting On the Answers

When you have answered these questions as specifically as possible in terms of your actual experiences and present feelings, reread them, perhaps several times, even aloud to yourself if that is helpful. From this rereading should emerge a clarified picture of what is taking place in your spiritual life and a growing sense of what your role must be in the unfolding story of your personal growth. Look for issues that you need to explore and decisions that suggest themselves. Are there different ways of behaving that you might want to try, some risks that look worth taking? What exercises learned in the course of journal keeping could be useful if applied now?

Working Together

Take turns sharing what you wish of your answers to the questions in this exercise. Offer insights, *not criticism*. In this discussion you will probably find some common items to focus on in future journal keeping and discussion, since this final basic exercise is at once a summary and a starting point, a taking stock of present attitudes which necessarily points in the direction of unresolved issues to be dealt with in the time to come. With your partner or group, make a list of the issues and experiences which you want to look at together. Decide which things you want to work on first and how you want to approach them, perhaps using strategies you have already learned from this introduction to journal keeping.

Recycling the Questions

As it is found here, this exercise is usefully repeated only at greater intervals. Perhaps a yearly taking stock of your sense of religious belonging is useful. The questions can be recycled, however, and applied to more specific religious subjects or to other areas of importance to you. You are, in essence, asking three clarifying questions: *What are my positive feelings about   ? What are my negative feelings about   ? How do I see myself in regard to   ?* You can use the questions repeatedly for a variety of subjects. Here are some examples: What are my positive/negative feelings about change in my Church — do I see myself as liberal, conservative, radical? What are my positive/negative feelings about where I live — do I view myself as a suburbanite, etc.? What do these views of myself do for me?

1

2

3

4

5

6

7

8

9

10

11

12

Conclusion

The exercise on religious belonging brings to a conclusion the first phase of the process of journal keeping. If you have actually begun to keep a journal with the help of these strategies, you have acquired a basic set of useful approaches to dealing with personal questions of belief and values, instruments which you can continue to use systematically for continued spiritual growth. Hopefully, working this way has brought you to the point of using your own imagination in order to raise provocative questions for yourself which also have become a part of your journal work.

I hope that by this time, your journal has become a spiritual ally and a trusted friend, that beyond the initial excitement of self-discovery, you have found in it a reliable way of taking counsel. If you have come this far you might take time out to read your journal as a whole up to this point, to get a larger picture of the you thus far contained in it, perceiving some of your rhythms, symbols and myths.

Where Do We Go From Here

Journal keeping can continue to provide a source of insight and growth. Working at it, you will improve in your ability to recognize and, if you are working with others, to express the significant events and feelings which call you to spiritual maturity. In them lies the daily bread of both mysticism and morality, the stimulus for truly organic change and improvements in your personal condition. Besides the ones contained in this little book, there are many other strategies which may be of help to you in meeting the wide variety of specific religious and moral questions which you must meet in the course of your spiritual journey. Some of these concern you alone; some include other people; some are concerned with the structures and institutions of religion and society. Make use of them whenever you find them. It is my intention to offer you more strategies specifically designed for the journal keeping process in the near future.

Cassette Program for Groups

Groups of persons who would like to learn the process of journal keeping should make use of the **Journal for Life** cassette program which has been designed as a companion to this book. It introduces the exercises and gives precise instructions about how to do them and share them in a group. The program is available from **Life in Christ,** 201 E. Ohio St., Chicago, Illinois 60611.

Appendix:

Some Guidelines for Discussing These Exercises With Others.

1. Don't Misuse Pronouns

Misusing pronouns has become such a common everyday experience that few people take note of it. Again and again I say "you" when I mean "I" projecting my feelings and experiences outward rather than owning, accepting, and taking responsibility for them. The frequent repetition of the phrase "you know" forms the punctuation of this language. Thus, I might say: "You know, you feel like nobody's going to give you a fair shake when you're looking for a job. They look at your hair and your clothes instead of your real ability to perform and, you know, your personality." Actually, the truth of the matter is that *I* am the one looking, seeking employment, and this has been *my* experience job hunting over the last couple of days. These misused pronouns are sometimes a direct source of confusion about what is being said and to whom. Most of the time, however, they subtly undermine conversation by diffusing ownership of statements. Something seems wrong or weak in the discussion but no one can pin it down.

"We" statements also tend to weaken the discussion by distorting responsibility and leading the group to false assumptions. "We feel," "we think" is often said when the speaker means "I feel," or "I think." Use of the word "we" requires evidence that others actually think or act in the same way as the speaker. In a group it generally means that the speaker who says "we" indiscriminately must be called upon to check out the assumption that others feel or think as he does by asking individuals if they agree. Similarly, "They say . . ." or, "Everybody knows that . . ." is a conversational red herring. The speaker who uses this phrase ought to be reminded either to assume authorship for what follows with an "I" statement, or be specific about whose opinion he is citing.Given the nature of the exercises in this workbook, individual experience is the focus of study. Misused pronouns are diametrically opposed to the learning experience. Group members should call each other's attention to habitual usage of such language, asking for restatement in a direct "I" form.

2. Don't Argue About Somebody Else's Feelings or Experiences

Statements which begin "Don't you feel that . . .?" undermine the authenticity of the sharing process. To contest someone's feelings or experiences because mine are different blocks my learning about the other and frustrates his attempt to communicate with me. Experiences may sound alike at times, but in the ultimate analysis they are the unique property of each individual. Accepting and arguing for only what fits my experience is unfair and unhelpful. Our objective here is to hear each other, but especially to help each other hear our own selves. We share in the group to hear ourselves better, to let others reflect what they hear coming from us. "Piggybacking," using another's experiences as a springboard to tell about my own is another form of contesting what the other person is saying. In addition it takes the floor away from the other. More obvious forms of "piggybacking" may begin: "I know exactly what you're feeling because I've had exactly the same experience when . . . " and, "that reminds me of the time . . . ." "Piggybacking" often indicates poor listening habits.

3. Avoid Leading Questions

Questions of the "Don't you think that . . .?" variety almost always mask a statement or opinion of the questioner. Like misused pronouns, they diffuse responsibility and destroy effective discussion. Persons who raise such questions should be encouraged to state their own opinion directly and then if they wish, solicit the opinions of others.

4. Avoid Analyzing

Much of the work you will do is directed toward helping you confront and own your own experiences and actions. Analysis, explaining things in terms of their psychological (e.g., "I keep rebelling against the world because I had a domineering father.") or economic or sociological dimensions, has a value of its own elsewhere. Here it tends to prevent growth and action by putting the focus elsewhere than on personal freedom and responsibility. Likewise in the group, avoid making analytic inferences about others' behavior, e.g., "You did this because . . . ." For your work here questions like, "What did you do next?" are much better than "Why did you do this?".

5. Be As Specific, Immediate, and Concrete as Possible

Abstract and philosophical statements are already judgments — they remove us from our experience instead of making it present so that we can learn from it. Data from the past is important when it is connected with how we feel and behave now, in the present. Avoid "storytelling." Being an entertainer is often a subtle way of attempting to get the approval of others while at the same time avoiding a serious look at one's self.